ACCOUNTABILITY AND YOUTH

*How We Can Take Charge of
Our Lives, Overcome Obstacles,
and Become the Role Models
Our Children Need*

Tony Howard

CONTENTS

INTRODUCTION

This book is the third in my series. Its main theme is: personal accountability and youth.

The most important thing to any of us is our children. In saying this, of course I mean my own child. But I mean yours too. I hope you agree that all children, not just our own, are our number one priority. I care about your kids and I hope you care about mine. Even if you don't have any children, the youth are the future of the human race and of the planet. What we do, we do for them.

Even apart from that sense of community, my kid lives in your world and your kids live in mine. We are all amazing, unique individuals, but "We're all in this together" is not just a slogan. We affect each other in very real ways. When I walk outside, I see kids. When my daughter walks outside, she sees adults. We see the people in our neighborhood and our community. My city is your city, my country is your country. What you do and what you look like affects my child.

Every person my daughter encounters on the street

becomes a role model, either for good or for bad. It's simply a fact. The better you act, the better the result on my kid. If you're nice to her, she benefits from that. She learns from your example. So the better your life is, the better teacher and leader you are, the better off all kids are.

It even goes like this for TV and the Internet—what our kids sees on their screens affects them in very profound ways. Who and what are they watching? Are they seeing shallow people talk about needing the most popular clothes and the most expensive cars? Are they watching impudent, bad-mouthed YouTubers and influencers constantly "roasting" or make fun of people? Or are they watching and absorbing positive lessons from people who measure success by happiness and the positive affect they have on those around them?

CHAPTER 1 - SENSE OF COMMUNITY

I've known people who measure success by how much more they have than their neighbors. "I got the fastest car on the block," they might say, or "my kids go to better schools than yours." These people might think they're winning because someone else is losing. But this is far from the truth.

How does it help me to help my community? Walk outside. Take your child. All you need to do is ask yourself this: which is better for my kid to see and learn from, a homeless person sleeping on the sidewalk or a successful entrepreneur running a local business? Which should they model themselves after, kids lazing around a street corner looking for easy money or an industrious youth out there putting him or herself through college by hustling a living, making deliveries, and cutting yards?

Which of these types of examples are going to give

your child someone to look up to, someone to emulate? We learn by example. So we must be careful who our examples are. And we must become the best examples we can be—not only for our neighbors' kids, but for our own.

Help with Opportunities

If outside my home there are teenagers cursing and tagging walls, my daughter witnesses it all. I try not to only recognize problems; I try to find solutions. I want to do something about it, but I need to take the approach with these teenagers that has the best chance of success.

I don't think it's ever the right thing to yell at these teenagers. That's not the right approach. All you will get is cursed at. If you yell at them, they will yell back. In fact, that's what I would do if I was them, especially if I was in front of my friends. In this case you can't fight fire with fire. It's just not productive.

So what do I do? When I see a kid spray-painting a wall, I hand him or her a business card. I tell them to call me because I have an opportunity to discuss with them.

Sometimes—not always, but sometimes—the youth will call me. Then I invite them to come to my office, at my school. They show up because they think I have a job for them. I don't. I tell them I see possibilities in them and that I want to help them with opportunities. So sometimes they come to my school thinking I have a job for them and they end up signing up for school. Sometimes they tell me they like the way I dress, that I look successful. They like my office; they're impressed with the school. Already, I've been able to inspire them by example.

I have helped get a lot of people off the streets, whether they're homeless people, people struggling with addictions, or people getting mixed up in crime or delinquency. I have learned that it's easier to help someone else than to use harsh words and then expect them to help themselves.

You can't help everyone. But if you try to help fifty people, it might stick with ten of them and make a big difference. Even one would be worth the effort.

Help by Being Positive
I see people on social media video themselves buying groceries for other people. I don't think it's the right thing to beg for this kind of attention and approval. That's why I'm writing these books and hope they can help some people—people can read them in private and not get stared at, not get embarrassed by seeking help and advice.

One time, years ago, I was out with a girlfriend at lunch. I went to use the rest room and my girlfriend said that she would pay the bill and treat me. When I returned from the bathroom, she went to the ladies' room. The waiter chose that time to come to me and tell me that my girlfriend's credit card didn't go through. He did it in secret, so that he didn't embarrass her. He didn't do it in a manner that alerted other people to it, and he didn't confront her about it and put her on the spot in front of me. I think this was a classy thing to do. She had simply missed a payment, but the way the waiter dealt with the situation, no one got hurt.

I think this is a great example of being positive. Part of being in a community is helping people. But always think about *how* you try to help. Will you drive people away or pull them in?

Be positive and don't point fingers. Don't embarrass people. Offer them help in a way that doesn't put them on the spot. Don't prejudge people. You never know what other people are going through. You never know what obstacles they're fighting against. Give them the benefit of the doubt.

Some people are victims of their environment. You can't go into a ghetto and walk around like you're going to solve everybody's problems. First of all, you don't get invited into someone's home and then go about rearranging the furniture as if you know best and they don't. And then, in some neighborhoods, if you do "the right thing," you get picked on. That's why I ended up, through trial and error, reaching out to people and trying to get them into a different environment, like my school, to meet up and talk. Get them into a place where they're surrounded by something positive. Let them see with their own eyes what an alternative might be. Give them a positive example.

You can't change people. They have to do that themselves. You can only recognize the possibilities and offer them opportunities.

Help Reduce the Crime Rate

Another way our kids are influenced by our community is through crime, or the lack of it. People commit crime because they're not financially stable, or because they lack direction. Maybe they're looking for a quick buck. Maybe they're repeating the mistakes of their parents. Some kids don't believe in themselves because they don't have anyone who believes in them.

If my kid walks outside and someone wants to harass her for money, it has an effect on her. If someone robs her or breaks into our house, it obviously has a very strong and immediate result. So the safer our neighborhood, the safer my daughter. This is a very concrete way that *your* positive sense of community benefits *my* child.

Kids in a variety of urban communities—rich and poor—see a lot of homeless people these days. I hand money to people. I know that money isn't always spent on worthwhile things like food, but I feel like I can spare a little, and so I do. People don't always pick up the phone and make a call when they see a homeless person unconscious on the street. More people call the SPCA when they see a dog outside on a porch in the cold. I believe we need to focus on the right things.

These are just a few ways in which I think we can put a focus on improving our communities. When you feel the urge to help people, that's a wonderful thing, but I suggest you be careful how you do it. When you see someone in need or someone heading down the wrong path, it's great to do something about it. But be sure you're not offending or embarrassing anyone when you do it. This is the best way to accomplish what you're trying to do. If you see crime or homelessness in your neighborhood, or youths misbehaving, remember this is not only your home, it's your child's too.

CHAPTER 2 - YOUTH IN CHANGING TIMES

We all know how times change. We all know older people who remind us that things aren't the same today as they were back in the day. I'm not exactly an old man but even I am here to say—these are different times than when I was young!

Because of the march of technology and personal devices, kids today are living in a whole new world. I remember going to the library to use encyclopedias. Nowadays, kids have Google. They have access to a world of information in the palm of their hand. These changes are like all changes—depending on us and how we use them, they can be good or bad.

The Good
Due to technology and all the information that is available to them immediately, I see how kids

today can better feed their imaginations. You're interested in how something works? Google it. You want a quick painting lesson? Go to YouTube. Curious about how a car engine works? Ask Siri.

Also because of technology, schooling has become more advanced. Resources are more readily available, and kids are surrounded by information more than when I was growing up. Kids today are doing math in the fifth grade that I was doing in ninth grade. I believe there is more of a focus on education in general these days. We may not see the positive results of this in all neighborhoods, but at least we're all talking about it more—so there are more opportunities.

I also believe that, because of all the devices and information surrounding them, kids today have a more entrepreneurial mindset. They are surrounded by more entertainment, more advertising, more images and visual stimulation. For instance, my daughter is always talking about ways she keeps herself busy. She comes up with great business ideas. I didn't have to work at it to keep her positive during the pandemic, she kept coming up with her own ideas when it comes to playing. She created her own puppets to entertain herself with, like her own version of The Muppets. She made these characters out of socks and glitter.

I know kids throughout the ages have been creative, but my daughter then approached her puppet characters like it was her own business, like it was an episode of Shark Tank. She didn't want me to interrupt her, she just wanted to talk and role-play the business.

She also realized that kids don't like wearing masks during the Covid 19 pandemic. She knew masks irritated kids so she set out to make customized masks for kids. I bought her disposable facemasks, and she drew on them. I wanted her to have fun with it but also learn, so we sold them at church, and I gave her the money. She felt great about it. She did something positive, making masks that kids were happier wearing—which in itself was amazing since it helped kids stay safe—and she also fostered her own entrepreneurial spirit. It was inspiring for me, seeing her create something smart that lifted people up, let kids have fun, and even helped save lives. All in all, it was a very positive experience. Without access to the Internet and TV, I'm not sure she would have taken these activities so far. So technology has its up sides, for sure.

The Bad
One bad side of kids having unlimited access to technology and devices is the potential for time wasting. Too much YouTube and TikTok—watching the wrong kinds of shows—can encourage kids to waste their time as well as witness and model bad behavior. Parental supervision and conversations with kids are very important.

I also believe that part of the information age means kids are seeing more luxury items and are watching influencers who encourage them to shallowly place a lot of value on fashionable material possessions for their own sake. On YouTube, for example, many times the role models are the kids who simply have the most "toys," meaning cars, jewelry, TVs, and other luxury items. It's easy for kids to get caught up in this and mix up needs with wants.

CHAPTER 3 - NEEDS VS WANTS

There is a big difference between a need and a want but sometimes they get mixed up. This has always been the case, but I think it's gotten more prevalent in the information age. Many people want what they can't get, see others who have more, and confuse "wants" with "needs."

Personally, I have a thing about TVs. How many TVs do people need? People take their 60" TV and toss it in their closet once the 70" ones come out. "Oh, that 70-inch is only $400 down at Best Buy this weekend!" they say. "I gotta have it! I need it!"

No. That's a want, not a need. I like nice TVs. I like big TVs. I want newest one too. But I want to save for my daughter's college fund even more.

I want to encourage my daughter to invest in her own future, to keep goals in mind, and not let money wash through her fingers. I want to help her appreciate the value of money. If you need to accumulate student debt, be smart about it. There's nothing wrong with a fast-food job if that's the best you can do at a certain time, but don't work a fast-food job and then spend a week's paycheck on a new TV. Save that money and invest it in your own future, whether it's schooling or your own business—so that months or years later, you're not working that same minimum wage job. Don't be someone who spends their money until there's nothing left but to complain about what they don't have.

And then, we don't always need the most name brand, luxurious item around. People think good means expensive but sometimes cheaper is better. Sometimes it's just common sense. For instance, I used to sell cell phone chargers. People would come to my kiosk, look at them, and say they're not great quality. I would ask them, "Why are you here?"

"My charger broke," they'd say.

"The one that came with it?"

"Yeah."

"Your $30 charger broke," I'd say. "Now you can buy mine for $5. In fact, I'll give you 7 for $30. You can use one after the other. They might break but —will they break any broker than your Apple one? And this way you'll have seven for the same price as one."

More expensive is not always better.

I believe everything happens for a reason. As awful as the Coronavirus is, as many people are tragically dying, and for all the pain it's caused—in another way it has brought us together. There is so much hate in our world and in our country today. Race, gender, Democrats and Republicans—we're so divided. Covid 19 doesn't discriminate. It kills everyone. Now we need to make sacrifices for each other. We need to take care of each other. We need to wear our masks, keep our distance, get our vaccines—we need to protect each other. As terrible as the virus has been, it has in one way gotten us back to what's important. It has reminded us about what is a need and what is a want.

Learn to recognize—and prioritize—your needs from your wants.

CHAPTER 4 - ROLE MODELS

As I mentioned, once your kids step outside, they're seeing role models—good or bad. The people they watch on TV or on their devices—they become role models as well. And of course, our parents are often our first and strongest role models.

For me, that was the case. My parents set the tone.

My mom was always the most beautiful woman in the neighborhood. She was known far and wide for her looks. But she was not a diva at home. She raked, she cut the grass, she watched over the family, and she got out and worked, too. She did whatever needed to be done. She rolled up her sleeves. She didn't rely on her looks. She didn't have a prima donna attitude and sit on the couch, making a man tend to her every whim. She was a true partner to my dad. Through all of these qualities, she taught me the values of humility, self-reliance, and hard work.

As a man, though, I suppose I saw my dad as an even

more influential role model. And he was a great one.

Dad worked hard. He was an electrician. But he always taught me the value of a backup plan. He was always finding ways to guarantee his family's safety and prosperity. And he was always working to improve himself and our family's condition.

We had a garden at home. Dad planted tomatoes, peppers, onions, all kinds of vegetables. As a kid, to be truthful, I was embarrassed by it. I was into basketball, not gardening. To me, the garden gave out an image like we were too poor to buy our own food. "Dad!" I'd say. "You got a good job! Why you gotta do that?" But that wasn't why we had that garden.

Dad had more than a garden, though. He had animals too. He bought goats. One time he even bought a cow. Let me tell you, if you've never had one, you don't know the behind the scenes of one cow! We had to feed it with a bottle. I was about 70 pounds, giving that cow a bottle and he used to pull on me something fierce, like he was saying, "Gimme that bottle!" I used to get mad at that cow, jerking me around like that. I hated this cow. One time I didn't feed it and it cried all night long—I mean *all night long*—and it was like he was telling on me.

"What's wrong with that cow?" my dad asked. "Did you feed it?"
"Yes, I did!" I lied to him.
But I couldn't BS my dad. He was measuring the feed!

17

We lived in Florida where natural disasters happened, hurricanes, floods, etc. The garden wasn't for fun. The goats and cow weren't pets. That cow got huge. Two years later, my dad had it butchered. That one cow filled up our deep freezer right to the top. We had a year's worth of meat off that one cow. I couldn't believe one cow had so much meat.

Dad earned a good living. But still he had that garden and those animals. It was one way to save money and that's one lesson I learned from my dad —it's always good to save money if you can, then redirect it into things for your own betterment. But more than that, the real point of Dad's "farm" was, if things go bad, if there's a natural disaster, you're going to need to survive. Those vegetables and those animals were a backup plan. If people rushed the grocery stores and there were shortages, we had food. If the roads were too bad or the stores themselves closed down for some reason, we had what we needed to live off.

It was a lesson in how to deal with life. Always have a backup plan. Nowadays I don't have a cow, but I know how to come up with solutions.

And also, today, I don't concern myself with what people think the way I did when I was a kid. Having a garden is a sign of preparedness and financial smarts. Thinking about Dad's garden is a reminder to me that we shouldn't assume everything is always going to be okay. We have to have backup plans. And we have to always work hard and never think we simply *deserve* to have nice things. We need to work to have nice things.

It's like credit—if you keep getting declined, you need an alternative. You need to work harder.

Having my dad as a role model paid off for me. I have to say, in the long run, Dad's lessons paid off for him, too. Today, Dad drives a nice car. He doesn't have any more cows. He eats out every meal because that's what he likes to do—and he's done well for himself. Today when people see my dad, they don't see that cow, they see his Mercedes.

CHAPTER 5 - COMPLAINING

I don't want to sound like your old great grandpa who walked three miles to school in the snow, but— I do think some of us these days blame other people for not handing us opportunities. In older generations, I believe people did not expect special treatment but instead sacrificed and *made it work.* They didn't sit back and blame people for not handing them free solutions.

I am the first to speak out against *any* type of discrimination whether its age, creed, religion, race, gender—you name it. However, for example, a complaint I hear a lot these days is that some people aren't getting the same treatment as others because of their background. I know these injustices are real. I know those things happen and they shouldn't. But there's a difference between fighting for what's right, and just throwing up your hands and giving up. There's a difference between spending all your time complaining, and spending your time advancing yourself.

I'm a Black man and I work in human resources. Statistically, not many men work in that field, and not many Black people, be they men or women. I don't complain about the fact that this puts the odds a little bit against me when I apply for a new job. If I don't get hired, I might think about it—how maybe if I wasn't a man or Black it might have gone my way. But I don't complain. Instead, I ask questions and I listen. If I hear that a certain certification will make me a more qualified and attractive candidate, I think seriously about going to get that certification. I don't complain about it, I go and do what makes me more attractive for the job, if that's my chosen field.

If I'm the wrong candidate for a job, I move on. I don't argue with the recruiter. I find another solution. I tell myself that the right job is still out there for me. I keep applying. I don't give up.

I know sometimes men like to hire pretty women. That's a fact of life. Again, I don't complain about that. I don't go home and sign up for welfare. I don't think about what's "fair" or what I "deserve." I listen to the feedback I get from the people doing the hiring and I work hard at making myself an undeniable candidate with the strongest qualifications. That's a big part of how I ended up with two graduate degrees.

Again, this trickles right down to our kids. Teaching children that everything has to be handed to them is not fair. It's doing them a disservice. We need to keep in mind the old school ways of respect, education, and good citizenship. We need to care about resumes and education. We need to constantly improve ourselves and keep thinking of ways to make us more attractive and productive workers. We need to pass these practices down to our children to best prepare them for their own careers.

Not everyone takes this stance.

I hear it more and more these days. "I'm not gonna get that job because they don't want no XXXXXX working there." You can fill in that XXXXXX with any number of words.

"Student debt is too hard to deal with," some people say, so they don't even try to go to school.

"Why can't I show my tattoos at my job? That's not fair!"

Other people complain about minimum wage and unemployment while they are refusing to work fast-food jobs or join the military or work outdoors.

You can't tell people you're suffering while you're being picky. *When it's life or death you do what you gotta do.* In the military I got yelled at. They screamed at me like I was a child. Did I like it? No way. But I saw the good the military was doing for me, so I took it. I took the bad with the good. The point is, you have to focus on what will work for you. You have to make sacrifices.

Instead of focusing on how student loans are too hard to pay off and complaining about it all the time, focus on how to pay it off.

For example, here during the Covid 19 pandemic, there's a lot of talk about the stimulus checks. Everyone feels they deserve one. Lots of people are fighting so hard for them. They make phone calls to the IRS. They take loans from friends saying they'll pay them back once the stimulus comes in. I see many people spending so much time talking about that stimulus money from the government that they make it a real focus of their lives.

The thing is, how far, really, will those checks go for you? Six hundred dollars, fourteen hundred dollars—people are spending so much energy talking about those checks, it's like they were a million dollars and were going to set these people up for life. The truth is—those checks won't really go that far. I live in southern California. Six hundred dollars just doesn't go that far. But lots of people love to complain about the stimulus checks and talk about them like they've won the lottery and are just waiting for the money to flow in.

And then, I know people who sat on their couches for a month waiting on their first stimulus check, complaining how late it was, and then once it came in what did they do? They ran out and bought themselves a PS4 gaming system. When the first $400 stimulus check arrived, I saw lines at the mall.

People were standing there waiting to get into designer stores like Gucci and Prada. Some of these were the same people complaining about food.

When the pandemic hit, I bought cases of Campbell's soup. My daughter knows I don't usually eat it and she raised an eyebrow or two but the thing is —those cans of soup are like my Dad's cow. This is what happens when things don't work in your favor. When worse comes to worst, this is how we prepare. This is how we survive. Why not focus on preparing yourself for hard times with what you *do* have instead of complaining about the government stimulus check you *don't* have.

There's also a big difference in *attitude* that comes from preparing with what you have versus complaining about what you don't. I'm sure you know people who complain a lot. Are they the happiest people you know, the ones always talking about what they're owed, what they are entitled to, what they're waiting on? No. The happier people are those who know in their hearts that they've spent their time and energy preparing for tough days that might be coming, the ones who feel ready for anything.

The flip side to this is that I know a lot of supervisors who are afraid to address problems in the workplace because employees sometimes make a big deal out of nothing. Employees are getting more and more used to complaining. Lawsuits happen. Managers have to walk on eggshells and then get afraid to take employees to task. As a result, the employees might start performing substandard work. This means the business suffers, the customer suffers with bad service, and even the employee suffers because they are learning and reinforcing a poor work ethic and job performance that will hurt their chances the next time they need a new job. Sounds like a vicious cycle, right?

What is the solution? I suggest that managers and supervisors need to be sensitive to their employees' needs, yes. But employees also need to understand that complaining about the small things is not the same as fixing the issues behind the small things.

CHAPTER 6 - PRIORITIES AND GAMING THE SYSTEM

Unfortunately, when it comes to income tax returns or government help or a stimulus check—it feels like once that money comes in, like I mentioned before, everybody needs to buy a big TV!

And the retail stores don't help. Why wait for Black Friday! Come down to Best Buy with that stimulus check because we're lowering prices! Wal-Mart and car dealerships do the same thing. When the stimulus checks arrive, the luxury items go on sale. People spend so much time complaining about how low the stimulus check will be—time they could have been working or building a business—but then instead of saving that money or investing it in themselves, they go and buy that 70" TV.

EBT is funding for low-income people to get food. It

used to be called food stamps, and they used to be actual stamps, but now the system has changed to where it's a card, like a debit card.

As a kid in the '90s, I grew up watching people exchange food stamps for real money. I watched people addicted to drugs exchange $100 in food stamps for $50 in cash so they could go buy drugs. People cry out that they need help and support, say they need money for food, and then they go and do that. Many of them have kids of their own. And as a kid, I watched that happen. What kind of example are these people setting for their own children? Or for the kids in their neighborhood? When people need help, we need to give it to them. But they need to be responsible with what they get.

My mom could have stayed home. She didn't. She went out and worked so we would have *more.* So our family could be *better.*

Finally the state smartened up a little and started giving out debit card instead of food stamps. But what did some people do? They started going out and buying food for other people. People would go get $300 of groceries on their EBT debit card—and then go sell them for $150 cash to someone. Now they have cash to, again, spend in unwise ways.

Nowadays you can use EBT at fast-food restaurants. This is money that is supposed to nourish a family and you can go spend it at Wendy's and McDonald's. Big Macs are not the right thing to spend that money on. You can even use it to buy electronics. You can go to a grocery store and buy whatever is in the store on an EBT card.

Of course Wendy's will take EBT. It just means more business. Fast-food places like that are basically the enablers.

There's nothing wrong with hard-working citizens complaining about this. But I do my best to come up with solutions. What we need are for smart, educated, experienced people to sit down together and come up with real solutions.

Off the top of my head, I say that if people are abusing the debit cards, don't give them a card. Let's have a government store where you go and there's a list of foods you can get, given your situation. Say you have four kids and you're a single mom. You get three cartons of milk, four packs of bread, etc. You get an inventory of food, based on you and your kids, that you can use for a month. No cigarettes, no luxury items sold inside the supermarkets, no BBQ grills or filet mignon—just the staples. Bread, meat, milk and such, so people can't sell it.

The system doesn't work properly, and the system responds to the issues rather than preventing the issues. We need different thinking. We need to get out in front of these problems. The fast-food corporations aren't going to complain. People who work there aren't going to stand up and say it's wrong—they'll get fired.

Again, the most important thing is setting the example for youth. That government store idea is just off the top of my head and I'm sure it has its problems to work out. But let's focus on an EBT solution and put our heads together. We can send rovers to Mars but we can't fix EBT?

Along the same lines, let's address child support. They should make child support go to the kid somehow. Right now, the mother can do whatever she wants with that check. It should be for rent, clothes, food—things the child needs. So many fathers complain that the mother uses the money for drugs, or on herself. In some cases, it's true. If you improved that system, you'd get more fathers doing the right thing and acting more responsibly. And of course, it would be better for the children, themselves.

CHAPTER 7 - APPEARANCES

We all need to do our best to *take advantage* of opportunities for ourselves. To me, part of this is a neat, professional appearance.

I'm known as the guy who wears the bow tie. It's my "thing" and I actually have about 300 of them. In this way, I stand out and people take notice of me. They remember me. On the Navy base where I've worked, I was always the best-dressed person on the base. And people knew me as the result. It wasn't the same type of reputation you get if you have, for example, some unique hairstyle or mustache. I was known to have a clean-cut, respectful appearance. As a result, my reputation automatically preceded me that I must have been a respectable person simply because I always looked respectable.

Also, strangers see me coming and immediately form a favorable impression. They see me coming a mile away in my bow tie. People are always saying to me, "Oh, you're so well dressed. You always look so nice." I can think of a worse way to be remembered. I can think of worse impressions to make. People on the street sometimes ask my advice and I think a lot of that has to do with my appearance. They call me "Mister" even though I'm not an older man. I dress to impress and people assume I'm successful. Also, because bow ties are not so common, they get curious about me. They ask me for help. It's sort of an icebreaker. So, because of my bow tie, I stand out and am more approachable, and I make an immediate good impression. Somehow, I'm an instant positive role model and it's not like someone like The Rock who's seen on TV—I'm someone right in front of people they can approach and feel good about. It's strange but true.

Also, it does *me* good to dress well. It changes me. I wear that tie and I'm forced to be professional. I stand out. I have to be good, my best. So just by how I dress, I have found, I have to set my own expectations higher. When I'm in jeans and a T-shit, I notice the difference. I have tattoos. When I don't wear long sleeves, I notice the difference. No one notices or cares how I act when I'm dressed down. But once that bow tie and slacks go on, I'm under the microscope and I have no choice but to be my best.

Again, I owe some of that to my dad. When I was a kid, my dad took me to my first job interview, at Hardee's. Before that interview, he took me to a clothing shop. He got me a button-up shirt, slacks, then tied my tie for me. I got the job.

If you look respectful, you are often treated with respect. If you look trustworthy, people often trust you. It's a fact. You don't need to break the bank. You just need to look presentable to leave a good impression.

I lift weights. I like how it makes me feel and how it makes me look. When I'm fit, people see it. And it gives me confidence. That is also part of appearances.

I like the California lifestyle. I like to relax in shorts and sandals as much as anyone. But there's a time for dressing down, and a time for looking good. I promise you, I wouldn't be where I am today if I left the house every day in shorts.

What's the better example for your kids? For youth in community? Someone in clean slacks and a bow tie, or someone in wrinkled jeans and a muscle shirt?

We lead by example.

CHAPTER 8 - MAKE THE BEST OF YOUR SITUATION

You want filet mignon. We all do. But if you can't afford it, what will you eat? Chicken breast. So what should you do? Complain that you don't want chicken breast? Spend your time moaning that you wished you had filet mignon? No. What you do is make that the best tasting chicken breast on Earth. Season it up. Make the best of it. Then save some money to buy and enjoy that filet mignon once in a while. Then make yourself work harder and smarter so that someday soon you can afford all the filet mignon you want and forget all about having chicken breast!

I was in the military. It was not much money, but it was stable. They give you a place to live, food to eat, clothes to wear. You might want more but you know how much money you're going to get every two weeks. That amount of money is not going to change. So you need to adjust your habits. Make a budget. Keep track of how you spend your money. Complaining about it isn't going to raise the numbers on that check.

Everyone's always fighting for a raise in minimum wage. There's nothing wrong with wanting more. And if you want life to be better, you need to fight for change. But it's not always about fighting for a higher minimum wage. If you want a better life, fight for a better job. Fight to build your own business. Get yourself in a position where minimum wage doesn't apply to you anymore. There's nothing wrong with working a minimum wage job. I promise you, I've done it. But I learned to fight for more.

California is a hard place to live. It's very expensive. I've been here for 20 years. The weather, the beaches —they're beautiful. But lots of people stay here and live three people to a small apartment because rent is so expensive. It's like college, living with roommates. Everyone's got their priorities but take a hard look at your circumstances. Are you spending too much on rent and still living like you're a college freshman? Is that the right situation for you? Are you making the most of your income and your expenses? If not, think about making some changes.

I really see three options if you're not happy with

your living situation in this light. Either leave it and move somewhere more affordable, work hard to change your situation and make more money, or simply accept it. But don't complain about it. Don't fill up your social media accounts with pictures of beach sunsets and then worry about how you're going to pay the rent.

Kids sense these things. Youth don't know right from wrong until they see it in their parents and other adults around them. If an adult complains all the time about their living conditions and doesn't do anything to change it, saying that they're being treated unfairly, the kids around that adult learns that complaining about unfair treatment is the right thing.

What happened to finding alternatives? Find a way to get higher certifications in your career and get a job that pays more money. If you can't afford a house, go live in a trailer. If none of those work, move out of L.A. if you can't afford it.

I've had to make sacrifices to live in southern California. I took on student loans to get my two master's degrees. But in the long run it makes me a more qualified job candidate. In the long run I'll make more money. I did this in order to live in California and be comfortable for my daughter and me. I didn't walk around complaining about how it's not fair that rents and mortgages in California are so high. I know exactly how much good that kind of complaining does—zero.

Make goals for yourself. Make budgets and projections. Be realistic. How much money do you need to live the lifestyle you want? Is it possible the way things are currently? If not, either change your income or change your expenses.

I was in the military and put my life on the line to have a stable living. if I could do that and come home safe, I thought, I can go to school and pay for my master's degrees to have a more secure future. I made my own calculations and figured that after thirteen years in the military and two graduate degrees, I felt like I deserved to make $150-200k per year. So that's what I work toward.

If I wake up one day and realize that I can't make that work, I'll go somewhere else.

CHAPTER 9 – COURAGE AND SACRIFICE

Courage

I served in the Navy for 13 years. I was overseas. I have seen bravery and courage. But I also know that bravery and courage come in all kinds of forms.

Sometimes courage means:
- To take shit from a manager, keep your cool and keep your job.
- To take on loans knowing it will pay off in the long run.
- To take the leap and start your own business.
- To put yourself out there for a job and face the possibility of rejection.

But these forms of courage are what we need to teach our kids that that's what it takes, and also that we'd do anything for them.

Sacrifice

Life is not meant to be all fun all the time. Who

wants to work? It's a sacrifice so at the end of the day, it's worth it in order to achieve a better life for you and your kids.

Instead of sitting at home complaining about how things aren't going well, we need to act.

Just about every person who works at McDonald's has a nice TV. I can't tell you how many homeless people I've met who have the latest cell phones. Many people who are jobless always seem to find a way to have iPads, cigarettes, and alcohol. This is not sacrificing. This is indulging in immediate gratification without a care for the future.

I went into the military because I couldn't afford college. The military paid for my school. That was the sacrifice. It was a long-term plan. I sacrificed my time and I risked my life, and I got the payoff. Not everything comes easy. Life is sometimes a process of give and take.

I decided at one point that I wanted to work in human resources. I had no experience so I took lower paying jobs in order to get experience onto my resume. I completed the certifications by investing my time and my money and having a long-term plan. Those are sacrifices. Like the military, they paid off.

Sometimes you need to put your pride aside. Don't let your emotions rule you. Emotion and pride are why someone won't take a job that they think is beneath them. But sometimes you need to dig deep before you can rise high.

It used to be that a high school diploma meant you could get a good job. Then it became a bachelor's degree. Now it's grad school. In the '90s if I had had two master's degrees, I would've thought I was Bill Gates. Always be humble, grateful, and appreciative. Be ready to make the sacrifices you need for your future.

In past generations, people went through some real hard times... Vietnam, WWII, the Civil War... segregation... maybe we don't think about it enough but some of these past generations had it ten times worse than us. People made sacrifices, sometimes even giving their lives, for future generations.

Now people raise a ruckus when their EBT cards don't work at all the fast-food restaurants. They complain that they can't show their tattoos on the job. We have something to learn from past generations about sacrifice. And always remember that we are also teaching our kids about it even when we don't mean to—by our example.

CHAPTER 10 – INSPIRATION AND MOTIVATION

Inspiration
We all need inspiration.

I mentioned the importance of my dad as my role model. Ever since I can remember, I saw how he was an inspiration to other people as well. People followed him. They listened to him. When I was nine years old, I said, "Daddy, you're gonna be a pastor one day. People like you. They come to you for advice."

Dad laughed when I said it. It sounded crazy to him. He was an electrician. Now, Dad's congregation only sees him as their pastor. They don't see the electrician, the gardener, the man who owned the goats and the cow—they don't see that. They only see how he is their pastor, their role model.

It's important for people to have role models. You see something you like about them and it inspires you to want to know how they got there, what they went through. You want to get to know them, personally. As I mentioned, I reach out to young people and once in a while I become a role model to kids. They ask me about my life. How I got to where I am. I tell them. I tell them about my successes and my mistakes. I try to be clear that they should learn from my mistakes. It's a responsibility every adult shares. Whenever we put ourselves in front of youth —we become a role model. My daughter loves Arianna Grande. She has inspired my daughter to want to be a celebrity and be able to influence people in a positive manner.

Motivation Not Decoration

I keep my place clean. I surround myself with a positive environment.

I have motivational things around the house. I keep items visible that inspire me and push me to make my dreams a reality. They are reminders of where I want to be.

I drink a bit every now and then but I don't keep alcohol out, on display. Instead, I keep fruit on the table. It reminds me to eat well. I see a banana or an apple on the table and I eat it. I keep healthy food in the fridge. I open the door when I'm hungry and eat what I see, and this way it's something good for me. That way, I don't need to hit McDonald's a little later.

I don't have photos of myself in my place. I have inspirational signs and posters. They say things like, "Be strong and courageous. Do not be afraid for the Lord, your God, will be with you." I keep that out where I see it every day.

I have some fake flowers. They're very pretty and they never die in case I forget to water them. To me, there is nothing pretty about a dead flower, but there's something nice about a fresh-looking bloom, even if it's not real. That's just me and you might be different. The point is, it makes me feel good to see them.

I have inspirational books out on a bookshelf. I keep some books out simply as reminders. I keep some textbooks out not because I need to read them again —I keep them out and visible because they are symbols and reminders that I need to always be improving and educating myself.

I have a record player. When I see it, I am reminded to embrace history. It reminds me how far we've come with technology. So I use it as a symbol, but I also listen to music on it. Music can make me feel good. I have both old and new records. Old songs tend to be romantic. They tend to be about love, not about sex. To me, that is inspirational.

I have mini globes everywhere. People see them and say, "Oh they're so pretty," but no, that's not why I keep them out. They remind me to keep in mind the whole world. They remind me that third world countries deal with so much more than we do. Think life is bad? Think about what life is like in countries that are still struggling and developing. The globes also remind me of the value of travel.

Sometimes I spin one of my globes, put down a finger, and see where it lands. Then I Google that place. I read about the place and what people do there, how they live. It helps me think outside the box. I don't stare down at a place like Jamaica and think how badly I wish I was there on the beach right now —I use the globes to educate myself.

I have exercise equipment in my place. I don't fold it up and put it in a closet when I'm not using it. I see it out and it reminds me to use it. I multitask. For me, my brain always needs to be moving. I'm better when I'm doing more than one thing. Plus, I can get more done. So I exercise while I'm on phone. Or I exercise while I have clothes in the washing machine.

It always makes me shake my head when I hear people say, "Oh, I'm busy washing clothes." How busy can you be when a machine is spinning your clothes around? Or someone might say, "Oh, I'm busy cooking." No! Mostly when you cook you might stir every five minutes. I do a little set of weights here and there. I stir, then I do a set. I put the clothes into the dryer, I do a set. I do some schoolwork for ten minutes, then I do a rep.

So for me, it's not about pretty pictures on the wall. It's about "decorating" my place with items that push me, educate me, act as symbols of what I want to achieve, and remind me of lessons I want to re-learn over and over.

CHAPTER 11 - MENTORSHIP

I have cherished the times I have had mentors. I'm prepared to have my faults pointed out. How else can I change my ways or improve? I see advice as an advantage. I am open to criticism. This is another form of courage. You have to be ready to receive criticism. Maybe you aren't ready to hear a particular piece of advice when you hear it. But maybe down the road you accept it. I've had moments where I think, "You know, that mentor was right. I need to work on that..."

Sometimes you are so caught up in yourself you don't see your faults. That's where a mentor comes in. Or sometimes another person may see something positive in you that you don't see yourself. Hearing them point it out can be a great benefit.

Say I went to a mentor and told them I wanted to be a firefighter. The mentor might ask me why. They might ask what was the reason behind the reason. "Okay," they might say, "But maybe what *else* do you want?" Sometimes it's the need behind the need. I might answer that I want to save lives. I like the re-spect of wearing a uniform. The mentor might dig deeper and open up other possibilities. It could be that I'm better suited to be a cop or a paramedic. Maybe I like protecting people. Maybe I like medi-cine. Maybe I don't really want to be a firefighter after all and it's better for me to find another way to help save people. So a mentor can help you find things you're good at, maybe even things you hadn't thought of yourself.

Mentors need to be realistic too. You can't save help or "save" everybody. Every mentor can only do the best he or she can. If I help one person, that per-son might help someone else—someone I couldn't help, personally. It blossoms outwards. I don't want people to look up to me and follow me. I'm looking to create leaders. I don't want my daughter to settle for a high school diploma. I want her to strive for more. I want her to be more successful than me.

As a mentor, one of the most important things I ever learned is the "80-20" rule. You let people talk 80% of the time. You only talk 20% of the time. If you let people talk, they usually will! Sometimes they'll vent. Sometimes being a mentor means: they talk out the pieces, you put together the puzzle. You need to make them believe in themselves. You need to give them a challenge.

Being a mentor has been good for me as well. You get challenged. You reassess your own beliefs. You are forced to seek out knowledge. Sometimes you never expect a certain question. You don't know the answer, so you find it out. That improves you. That was something I didn't expect until I mentored people—that it would make *me* the one who learns something. I strongly recommend mentoring people. Again, the focus of this book is youth, and mentoring is a great way to help out—and help yourself.

As a mentor, people believe in me *so* much. They see the potential in me. It helps with my confidence. It keeps me striving to be my best. It's like they're mentoring *me* with the faith they put in me and it's a great thing.

Someone told me I should talk more about how people can improve their credit when I'm mentoring. It made me stop and think. I said, "Hey, let me do that for myself! Let me improve my own credit!" So off I went to learn more about it. It had a positive effect on me.

CHAPTER 12 - DREAM BIG BUT BE REALISITIC

I was director of admissions at a school. It gets pretty easy to detect lies when people come in to apply to the school or interview. Most of the time you just can't BS people. If you can't do math, you won't be a doctor. If you can't stand up and feel comfortable in front of people, you won't be a public speaker. Don't lie to other people, or to yourself, when it comes to your plans for the future. Be realistic.

Don't just say I need a great job. Be specific. Is it realistic to say you're going to play the lottery and win? No. You need a plan. A realistic plan.

You want to buy a house? Think about how you will do it. So many things go into buying a house. Research it. Figure it out. Is it doable at the moment? What do you need to get there?

How many people who work at McDonald's actually

go to Dubai for vacation? Maybe think about Hawaii instead if you live on the West Coast. Dream, but create believable dreams. If you want something to be a reality, choose something doable. My car was my friend's dream car. For her, it was everything. For me, it wasn't a big deal. Everything is relative and we all need to look at our goals through the lens of what is actually possible, not a pipe dream.

I'm tough on people. I couldn't teach elementary school. I think many of those kids would end up crying in my class! That's one of my limitations and I embrace it. But I believe that being realistic helps people get to their goals. I pat you on the back when you deserve it. I don't yell at you, but I tell you like it is. You want to go to Dubai? Great. Can you afford it right now? No? Then save up and go to Hawaii. Then go back to school, land a better job, and a few years from now, go to Dubai once that is a reality. Don't give up on Dubai. Always aim your dreams high! Just keep it real. You want to be a doctor but you don't get great grades? Strive for it. Hope for it. Figure out what it will take to get there. But be okay with the idea that you may end up an RN or a medical assistant if your grades just don't get there. You need to dream big but you need to be realistic.

Me, I can't teach kids. But I can kick some adults in the butt and try to do them some good, so that's what I strive to do.

CHAPTER 13
- MISTAKES

I've made tons of mistakes. My mistakes define the man I am today. I can relate to people because of them. True influencers are people who have been there and done that.

I have made business mistakes. I sold my house after I got out of the Navy. I took the money and bought five small businesses. I jumped into them without knowing the industries. I just wanted my own businesses. I didn't know things like employee law and employee handbooks. I hadn't educated myself. I ended up in lawsuits that didn't exactly feel good or turn out in my favor!

I needed that kick in the ass to learn from. I had to pay—both "my dues," and I had to pay, literally. Sometimes you get so caught up in it, you make mistakes. I wasn't disciplined.

So I took some advice, I sold my businesses, and I educated myself about employer-employee relationships and the law. It was good because it pushed me to go back to school to learn some specific things you need as an employer and entrepreneur. Then one thing led to another and I ended up in human resources! I learned so much about employee issues that I became an expert in it all! I'm now a contract specialist. I never saw that coming but that's how one thing leads to another when you're on the right path. One big mistake actually pushed me in a new direction.

CHAPTER 14 - SINGLE MOMS

Single moms are a group I have a certain soft spot for. As a group, in my humble opinion, I think there are some things they might benefit from keeping in mind.

There are a lot more single moms out there today than when I was a kid. This is something young women want to think about very seriously. My daughter is the best thing in my life. But for young women, there is a time for having a child and a time for focusing on career. There is such a thing as getting a fresh start and building a life that is conducive to raising a kid, comfortably for both the mom and the child.

Everyone has sympathy for single moms, and for good reason. Many of them face tough challenges, I know. But there is always a way to make it work. And it's never productive to point fingers at the system, or at the father—focus on changing what you have control over.

If you are a single mom with one child, think hard before having your second, third, or fourth child. What are your goals and priorities? Is it the right time? I'm all for kids! But I do encourage young women to be realistic about the timing, and about the long-term benefits of having them now versus having them later.

Motherhood is beautiful. It teaches responsibility. It brings us the joy of family and children. But there are also negative repercussions of motherhood when the timing or the attitude isn't right.

If a woman is on welfare, getting pregnant is not usually the right move. There's a time to work on yourself, and a time to dedicate your energy to a child. A child will be happier and better off if the mother has already taken the time to establish herself with a career. If she is stable. People need to hold themselves accountable, especially when children are concerned.

I know some single mothers whose first excuse for not advancing themselves outside the home is: I want to work but I need to watch my kids and I don't have any support from the dad. In this situation every single mother needs to understand the opportunities and support out there.

If someone needs to be home, they can always take online classes. No one says you need to go to a university for four years to get a degree leading to a job.

When your kids are in school, *you* can go to school. I used to take online classes when I was working full time. It was a lot easier than taking the time—which I didn't have—to drive to a school.

You can take online vocational courses. In many cases, after six months, you have a certification. There are also ways out there to find grants and financial aid if money is tight. I used to work at a vocational school and some programs are as low as fifty to one hundred dollars a month. I think just about anyone can make that happen.

If you want something, you need to pay into it. You need to take risks and make sacrifices. Just be sure to be realistic with your job goals. It might not be the time to set your sights on being a doctor, but if you love the medical field and helping people that way, why not look into courses that prepare you for important and in-demand jobs like nursing assistant, laboratory worker, or medical machine technician, etc.?

Medicine is just one example. There are courses out there for business administration, information technology—loads of possibilities. Take it one step at a time. Just aim to get your foot in the door at first. Maybe you put yourself on the path to getting a job that doesn't start out making a lot of money, but you get your foot in the door. One thing always leads to another.

Choose an industry that interests you. Aiming toward a good paycheck is always important, but no one wants to work every day in a job that holds no interest for them. Ask around, find someone who works in this field and educate yourself on the realities of working in that field. As I discussed earlier in this book, a good conversation with a mentor can go a long way. Maybe some new field of study you hadn't thought of will pop up. That's how I got into human resources. I never would have landed there if I hadn't listened to a mentor, taken that first class, and experimented in a field I didn't even know I was interested in.

Another great option for single mothers is getting into childcare. I think this is an opportunity that many single mothers should consider. If you have kids, there's a good chance you like kids! If you're spending your time watching your kids, feeding them, consider watching other kids as well. Finding quality childcare where I live in San Diego is difficult. They fill up, they're expensive. It's one field that will never dry up! People are always having kids! Talk about job security.

Why not explore opening your own childcare business, or go work at one? That's what I would do if I were a single mom. You can charge good money, have job security, and work with kids all day. It doesn't have to be fancy. Take a business course and see if starting your own business is for you.

When people are struggling, they can do a lot more

together than alone. Find other single moms and band together to open a childcare facility. If you need to take a business course, don't look at it like a burden or like debt—it's an investment. You need to put in work to start a business like daycare but it will pay off in the long run.

Because I enjoy writing, I often suggest writing to people as well. Single moms can write about their experiences, their struggles. Share them. Let everything you do count. Maybe you can inspire other mothers and give them support. Maybe it can lead to making money off your writing. Let all your struggles become positive somehow. Look for ways to turn them good.

There are loads of home businesses you can create. Are you creative? Can you work with your hands? Do you like crafts? Think of ways to turn those interests into income. Make candles and sell them on Etsy. There are twelve-year-old girls on Etsy making slime in their mother's kitchen, tying it up with pretty bows, and selling them off for $20 each! The opportunities are there. Turn a hobby or a passion into income. What are *you* good at?

If you're a real go-getter and motivated to work on your own, try door-to-door sales. There are loads of companies out there you can work for. Some of them sell quality products you can be proud to offer. You can make your own hours and one of the great things is—the harder and smarter you work, the more money you make.

Another self-starter business is housekeeping. All of us can clean a house. Turn that into income. Start your own cleaning business. You might not like the sound of this, but it's called sacrifice. It's also possible to start the business yourself, grow it to where you hire people, and pretty soon your employees are doing the cleaning and you're sitting home on the phone taking orders.

Single mothers can always consider going into the military. Joining the military doesn't have to mean leaving home and going to live on a base or overseas. You can be a reservist. You can get job training. You get medical and dental insurance, shelter, a paycheck, establish credit. And, you're serving your country. When I joined the military, I was scared as hell. My chest was all caved in. There came a day pretty fast when my chest puffed itself out and I started believing in myself. It's all positive.

So single mothers really have lots of opportunities. Sometimes we just need to be reminded of them. A good mentor can be invaluable for this. Sometimes we can turn our passions into income. Be creative and be open to new ideas. Think outside the box. Keep your eyes open for good idea and for opportunities. Work doesn't have to be a chore. The lucky ones among us find work they can do, even from home, that earns us money and makes us proud of what we do. What better example can a single

TONY HOWARD

mother be to her kids?

CHAPTER 15 - COMING OUT OF PRISON

I spend a lot of time with people who have been in prison. They face their own unique challenges and I would like to address them, like single moms, specifically.

The biggest challenge for men and women coming out of prison is that they're limited in their options. This is not something you can fight against. You need to understand it and be realistic.

Coming out of prison, you're not going to get your dream job right away. One year later, you're not going to be a doctor, a lawyer, or probably not a school teacher either. Let's not waste our time.

People need to dream but coming out of prison, people are best off dreaming about something that can actually happen. They need realistic expectations. I asked my daughter at eight years old what she wanted to do when she grew up. She said she wanted to be rich. Then she said, "I want to be famous." These answers are fine for a child. I will never shoot down anyone's dream. But for a thirty-year-old coming out of prison, being rich and famous is not a realistic plan. Aim for those things if you want them. That's great. But make a living first. Be successful first.

You were in prison learning from your mistakes. How can you turn that into a positive? Now you're someone who can talk about turning negatives into positives. You can be an author or a speaker. You could get a job working with people who have had similar experiences to your own. There are even people I know who make a living bringing literature, art, or theater to prisoners.

You can always turn a negative into a positive. A mentor of mine used to say, "Be an expert in something you were a failure at."

Did you have a problem with drugs? Go talk to people about it. Be an activist. Did you damage your own relationship with your kid? Help other people form and improve their relationships. Help them learn from your mistakes. If something set you back, let it become a passion and use it to help other people.

My brother was in prison. When he got out, he started cutting grass for a gardening company. I was proud that he got himself honest work. I applauded him. I also started telling him immediately to save his money, get his own lawn mower, and work for himself.

Go do labor work in a field you enjoy. Do you love cars? Work for a mechanic. Learn from him or her. Learn how to refurbish cars. You never know where it leads. Do well at one job, prove yourself, and someone might offer you something better. It's happened to me and it's led to some surprising job opportunities I never expected.

By now you probably know that I try and push people toward working for themselves. You can be an entrepreneur and work for yourself. This is an opportunity to generate money and work without a background check. Again, be realistic. And hustle. Just about anyone can wash a car or be a gardener. Don't be too proud. Strive to grow your business. It's possible that soon enough you're hiring other people to do the harder work while you're managing the business if you don't like the work itself.

In my honest opinion there is an amazing opportunity for people coming out of prison. It might sound funny to hear, but you have a fresh start. You can look at yourself and figure out what you are good at or what you enjoy, and work to turn that into your own business. It's similar to the advice I give single moms. Start small. Think about housekeeping, cutting grass, painting houses. Maybe start out working for someone else—but find a way to save. And always consider starting your own business when the time is right. It won't happen overnight. But you have the ability to be your own boss in the industry of your choice, build something for yourself—and be a great role model for the youth.

No matter which path you take coming out of prison, always remember that no one owes you anything. You need to fight for it, earn it. Give people a reason to believe in you. The world is not fair. This might be tough to hear but it's true.

Have discipline. Dress well. Get yourself a good haircut. Think about the image you present. People should accept you for who you are, yes, but there really is such a thing as making a good impression.

I cover up my tattoos in professional settings because I want to be taken seriously. I don't take the chance they give people a negative image. Always be presentable. Don't scare people off with your clothes or your image.

Be ready for rejection because you will get rejected. Don't give up. Go work fast food if you have to. Take that job if it's the best thing you have going. But don't stop there. That job is not your goal. Start your own business. Go to school. Invest in yourself. But also be realistic. Lots of men coming out of prison want to be mechanics. When I hear that, I offer some advice. Go study HVAT work: heating and ventilation. Do that *now*. Do cars *later*. If you love cars, that's great. Be successful and make money and get on your feet with something that has great pay and job security and not enough workers—and *then* go back and learn about cars. Make the money the most guaranteed way possible first. HVAT is a great field and workers are pretty much always in demand. Or learn about electricity. That's another great field. The mechanic and car-refurbishing field is limited and full of experienced workers. Go where the money is. Sacrifice for the future.

The best thing is to create multiple careers. Learn HVAC, work in landscaping, be an author—give yourself various streams of income. And of course, once you're ready, whenever possible—work for yourself.

CONCLUSION

When we improve ourselves, we improve our community. When our kids step outside, they are faced with role models, good and bad. There's no other option—it's just the way it is. The better role model I am, the better my community is, the better my kid is, the better all kids are, the better community *they* build when they grow older. It's one big cycle and we're all part of it.

We all want a better life for our kids. Hopefully we all want a better life for all kids, not just our own.

Courage, mentorship, leading by example, appearance, realistic goals, sacrifice, recognizing the difference between a need and a want, preparing for the future, always trying to improve the system— these are things that can make me a better person so that I can be a better role model for all kids—mine and yours.

I think if you look at this book as a whole, what I'm trying to say is—it comes down to personal accountability. We can't just complain about our life. We have to get over that hurdle. We have to act.

We have to look at our neighbor and help them if we can. If we let them sink, they will drag us down with them. The more crime, the higher the taxes. We need to help our neighbors and help all children because it is the right thing to do for them—but also because it is the best thing to do for ourselves, since what lifts them up lifts us up as well.

It's not always easy. But it's always worth it. We all need to live up to our potential and give ourselves the best possible future—for ourselves and for our children. Help yourself, and you help the youth. Be a better person, and you're a better role model.

Those are the best ways I can think of to help build a better world for my child—and for yours.

ABOUT THE AUTHOR

Tony Howard

Tony Howard, Founder and CEO of Redefine Works, writes from his wide range of experiences in education, business, and the US Navy. Behind Redefine Works is Tony's unique principal that at any given moment, by clarifying what we want and who we really are, we can change the way we interact with the world and adapt to changing circumstances through our own personal rebranding, thereby pursuing new passions, and improving the lives of others as well as ourselves.

Tony studied business at the University of Phoenix and holds two master's degrees from Argosy and Brandman Universities.

Tony points to his daughter as the guiding light of his life, gives all grace to God, and thanks all those who have supported and believed in him. Tony calls California home and can often be found walking the beach, refurbishing classic cars, and exploring local museums and zoos.

ACCOUNTABILITY AND YOUTH—How We Can Take Charge of Our Lives, Overcome Obstacles, and Become the Role Models Our Children Need—is Tony's third book.

Made in the USA
Middletown, DE
08 October 2022

12226212R00046